All About Animals

Zebras

By Christina Wilsdon

Reader's Digest Young Families

Contents

Chapter 1
A Zebra Story

Mane Event

A baby zebra's mane runs all the way down its back—from its ears to its tail! The little zebra loses most of the mane on its back when it is a few weeks old.

A herd of zebras graze on an African grassland. Their tails swish, flicking away flies. The zebras look up curiously as one female walks away from the group. Then they drop their heads and continue grazing.

Father Zebra, however, follows Mother Zebra. She is about to give birth, and it is his job to stand guard nearby.

Carefully, Mother Zebra lies down. Her baby is born quickly. She jumps to her feet, then nuzzles her new foal. She licks him with her big tongue.

Ten minutes later, the baby, too, is on his feet. He sways on his long, skinny legs. Just half an hour later, he is able to walk—and fifteen minutes after that, he can run! Now he can flee with his mother if a hungry lion chases them.

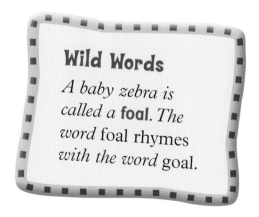

Wild Words

A baby zebra is called a **foal**. The word foal rhymes with the word goal.

Mother Zebra leads her baby back to the group. She shields him from the other zebras, kicking and nipping any that come near. She will not let her baby get to know the other zebras for a few days. First he must learn that she is his mother.

A week passes. The baby grows plump from drinking his mother's rich milk. Sometimes he nibbles on grass, but milk is his main food until he is six months old.

The baby zebra stays close to his mother, but as he gets older, he leaves her side now and then to play with other foals. They romp and kick, rear and race. Their favorite game is chase. They even chase birds and other animals!

Baby Stripes

Baby zebras often have brown and white stripes when they are born. They are also fuzzier than their mothers.

By his first birthday, the baby zebra has become a big, strong colt. He can take care of himself. But he still follows his mother, who has just given birth to a new baby.

Some colts stay with their family group until they are four years old. But one day, the colt's brothers leave to form a small group of their own. The colt dashes off with them, kicking and play-fighting as they go.

The mare's new baby is a female—a filly. She will stay with her family until she is about one and a half years old. Then she will go off to join another stallion's herd of mares, spending the rest of her life with them.

All Grown Up

A filly usually has her first baby when she is about two and a half years old. A colt does not become a stallion with his own herd until he is about six years old.

Chapter 2
The Body of a Zebra

A zebra becomes a blur of black and white as it picks up speed to escape the wildebeest and cheetah that are chasing it.

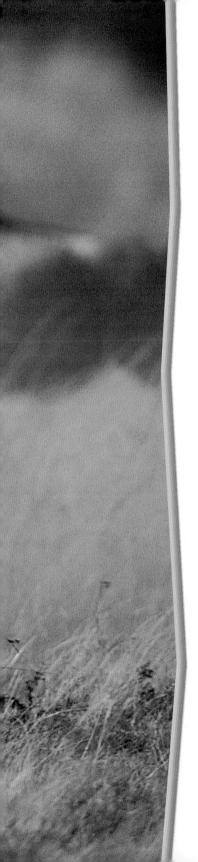

Racing Stripes

Zebras are wild cousins of horses and donkeys. The most common kind of zebra—the plains zebra—is about the size of a big pony. A stiff mane sticks up from its neck like bristles on a brush. Wide stripes march down its neck and body and loop around its rump.

Like horses, zebras depend on speed to escape predators. A zebra can gallop at nearly 40 miles per hour—that's more than double the speed of a very fast human runner. Big muscles bunched up at the top of its legs give the zebra its power. Strong fibers in its legs stretch, helping the zebra spring forward as if it were leaping on pogo sticks!

A zebra can flare its nostrils wide to gulp down air, and a big chest helps it take deep breaths as it runs. The extra oxygen helps the zebra run faster.

Shoo, Fly!

A zebra's tail is 20 inches long. It makes an excellent flyswatter! A zebra can also twitch its skin to shake off flies.

Alert for Danger

Zebras are a favorite meal of lions, leopards, hyenas, cheetahs, and wild hunting dogs. Zebras watch carefully for these predators.

The location of the zebra's eyes help the zebra to spot danger. The eyes sit on the sides of its head, which allows the zebra to see behind it and in front of it at the same time without twisting its neck! The eyes are also placed high up, so the zebra can see what's going on around it even when its nose is deep in a patch of grass!

If a zebra spies a lion, it snorts loudly. It may turn and face the lion and even stamp its hoof. Other zebras may join in. Then the lion knows that the game is over. It has lost its chance to launch a surprise attack!

Beautiful Dreamer

Zebras aren't always on the alert. Like all animals, they need to sleep. One zebra stands guard while others rest. This zebra's half-shut eyes show that it is taking a nap. A zebra can doze while standing because its legs lock in place to hold it up. But at night, zebras may lie flat on their sides to sleep.

Zebras use their keen vision and hearing to check for danger. Their big, cupped ears swivel in all directions to catch the smallest sound!

Each zebra has its own voice, and other zebras in its family can recognize it by sound alone!

That's a Mouthful!

Grass isn't an easy food to eat. It is stringy and tough. But a zebra's teeth are up to the job. A zebra gathers grass with its long, rubbery lips. Then it grabs the blades with strong, curved teeth at the front of its mouth. With a jerk of its head, it rips off the grass tips. Its big tongue shovels the grass deeper into its mouth. Finally, the broad teeth in the back crush the grass. Ridges on the teeth grind it into pulp. The zebra's jaws go around and around as it chews.

Chewing grass wears down teeth. A zebra's teeth, however, are long and deeply set in its jaws. They slowly push up and out from the gums so that the zebra is able to continue chewing throughout its life.

Sounding Off

Zebras don't neigh like horses, but they are noisy! A plains zebra calls to other zebras with a loud barking, whistling bray. Baby zebras squeal. Fighting zebras squeal and grunt. A relaxed zebra blows air out of its nose and mouth with a fluttering sound.

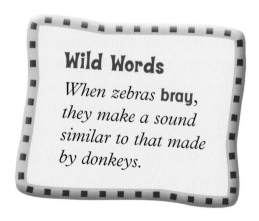

Wild Words

*When zebras **bray**, they make a sound similar to that made by donkeys.*

Chapter 3
Zebra Stripes

Take a close look at the three plains
zebras in this picture. Can you see
how their stripes differ? Each zebra
has its own special pattern of stripes,
just as you have your own fingerprints.
No two zebras are exactly alike!

Stripes Galore!

The first thing we notice about a zebra are its stripes. No other animal, not even its close cousin the horse, looks anything like a zebra. Its bold pattern led to its nickname, "tiger-horse."

At first glance, zebra stripes look alike to us. But there is an astonishing variety of stripes! Plains zebras have big, bold stripes. Other kinds of zebras have thinner stripes—and more of them. The thinnest stripes belong to the Grevy's zebra. It has over twice as many stripes on its body than a plains zebra. Some Grevy's zebras have reddish brown stripes. Mountain zebras have thinner stripes than a plains zebra, but they have thicker stripes than a Grevy's zebra!

Tail End

Each kind of zebra looks different from the back. The stripes on a Grevy's zebra whirl in circles around its tail. A patch of white surrounds the wide black stripe on its back. A plains zebra has stripes ending in triangles pointing at its tail.

Grevy's Zebra

Plains Zebra

Strange Stripes

Some rare zebras are striped in reverse! They are black where they should be white, and white where they should be black. They look like black horses with thin white stripes. Some zebras' stripes blend together so that they look black with white spots. An albino zebra has no black at all. It is white with beige stripes.

Striped Clues

A zebra's stripes are a clue to where it lives. A zebra of the northern plains has black and white stripes. Its legs are striped all the way down to its hooves. A zebra from the south has dark stripes, but they are not pitch-black. They may even be brown. The lower parts of its legs are white, not striped.

Shadow Stripes

Some zebras of the southern plains have pale stripes in the white spaces between black stripes. These are called shadow stripes. They can be seen on this zebra mare's rump and sides. Her foal has shadow stripes, too.

Even a zebra's mane is striped. The stripes on the neck of this Grevy's zebra reach up into its stiff mane. A mane helps protect a zebra's neck from bites by other zebras. Some plains zebras do not have manes at all. Sometimes a whole herd may be without manes. Sometimes just the stallions lack them.

Stripes may help protect zebras. When zebras race across the plains, their stripes become blurry, making it more difficult for a predator to focus on just one zebra.

Why Do Zebras Have Stripes?

Some scientists think stripes help zebras escape predators. A herd of zebras turns into a swirl of stripes when it runs. This might confuse a predator and make it hard to single out one zebra in the crowd. But other scientists point out that lions do not seem to be confused by zebra stripes.

Stripes do break up the shape of a zebra. It is easier to see a wildebeest's dark body from far away than a zebra's striped body. But that is only if the zebra is standing perfectly still—and zebras do not freeze when they see a lion!

Perhaps stripes help keep zebra families together. Zebras recognize their family members' stripes, and baby zebras bond with their mothers' patterns. However, horses have no problem recognizing other horses even though they lack stripes. Why should zebras need them?

Stripes may help ward off insects. Scientists have found that a pesky insect called the tsetse fly would rather land on dark animal skin than light or striped skin. But zebras do not get sick from the bite of a tsetse fly—and they still get bitten by other insects.

So why do zebras have stripes? We may never have a black-and-white answer to this question!

Chapter 4
Zebra Herds

One zebra stands guard as the others drink at a water hole. All the zebras have their ears pricked to listen for danger – lions may be hiding nearby and crocodiles may be lurking underwater.

Families Together

Huge herds of zebras graze on the African plains. In the wet season, they stay in one place to eat fresh, new grass. In the dry season, hundreds of zebras trek across the land to find food and water.

These big herds are made up of many small zebra families. Each family includes a stallion (the male), a few mares (the females), and their foals (baby or young zebras). Foals in one family play with foals from other families, but the mares do not mix. Mares in different families will even snap at one another if they get too close! Stallions greet other stallions by sniffing noses, then rearing and jumping away.

Why do all these families herd together? Because for zebras, there is safety in numbers. Many pairs of eyes looking for danger help all the zebras stay alive. And when predators do attack, it's safer to be part of a thundering herd than off on one's own or in a small group.

Neighbor-Herds

Zebras often form large herds with other kinds of animals. Wildebeest, gazelles, and giraffes are common companions. Warthogs, elephants, and even ostriches may be part of the herd, too. Herding together helps all the animals—it means more eyes, ears, and noses on the alert for predators!

Zebras, wildebeest, and gazelles all eat grass, but they do not compete for food, because each one grazes differently. Zebras eat the top parts of grass blades. Wildebeest graze on shorter grass. The little gazelles nibble on new grass.

All Aboard!

Oxpecker birds often ride on zebras' backs. Sometimes a zebra may carry more than a dozen of them—and even have birds hanging off its sides and belly! Zebras have a two-way deal with oxpeckers. The birds clean pesky bugs off the zebra's skin and get a meal at the same time. A zebra knows a predator is near when the birds hiss and fly away.

Zebras take their turn at a water hole after the wildebeest are finished. The zebras stay close to shore in case a crocodile pops up with open jaws!

Each mare in a herd has her own place in line. Young zebras walk behind their mothers. If a mare tries to cut in front of another zebra to move up in line, the other mares kick and bite her until she goes back to her place!

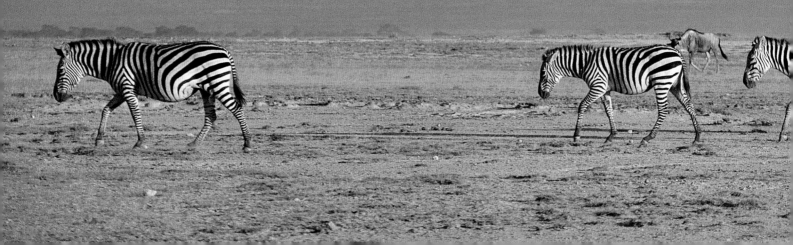

Getting Along

The stallion is the leader of a zebra family. He chases other stallions away from his mares and foals. A stallion also protects his family from predators. He runs in between his family and a predator and also stands behind them at water holes.

One mare helps the stallion manage the family. She is often the oldest mare. She always walks in front of the other mares to lead them on trails, with the stallion last in line.

The mares in a family form close bonds with one another. They stay together as a family even if the stallion dies and a new stallion takes over.

You Scratch My Back, I'll Scratch Yours

Zebras spend hours grooming themselves and one another. Two zebras often stand side by side, head to tail. Each zebra grooms the other's neck and back. This helps zebras clean parts that are hard to reach. By facing opposite ways, they can also watch out for danger in all directions.

Chapter 5
Zebras in the World

Where Zebras Live

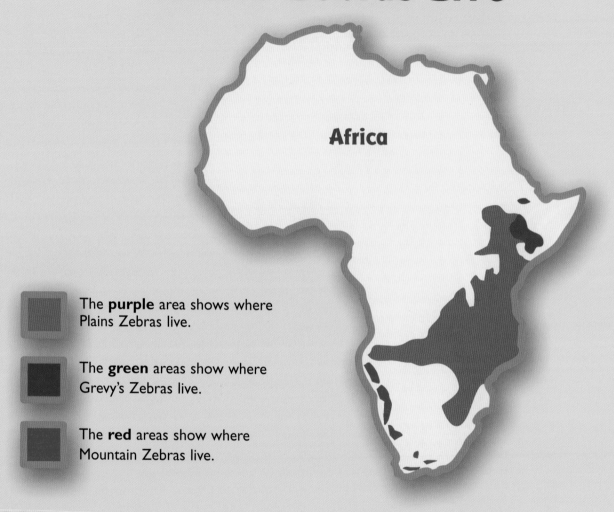

Africa

The **purple** area shows where Plains Zebras live.

The **green** areas show where Grevy's Zebras live.

The **red** areas show where Mountain Zebras live.

Zebras of the Past

Just over 100 years ago, there lived a kind of zebra called the "quagga." Quaggas sported red-brown stripes on their heads, necks, and shoulders. They had red-brown bodies and white legs. But by the late 1800s, they were extinct. Europeans had hunted them for their hides and had taken over their grasslands so that cattle could feed there instead. Laws now protect zebras.

Zebra Habitats

There are three main types of zebras. They live in different habitats in Africa.

The most common type is the plains zebra that lives on the plains and the savanna. A savanna is a grassland that also has trees. Plains zebras range from southwestern to eastern Africa.

The Grevy's zebra lives in dry grasslands and deserts. It can be found in parts of Kenya and Ethiopia in eastern Africa. Grevy's zebras do not live in herds. They live alone or in small groups that do not stay together for long.

Mountain zebras live in hilly parts of Angola, Namibia, and South Africa. These little zebras have hearts that weigh more than a plains zebra's! Extra-powerful hearts help pump blood at high altitudes where there is less oxygen in the air.

Zebras Big and Small

Of the three types of zebras, the smallest is the mountain zebra. It is about 4 feet high at the shoulder. The biggest is the Grevy's zebra, shown here. It can be as big as a full-grown horse.

The Future of Zebras

Today the plains zebra is plentiful and is not in danger of extinction. But two other kinds of zebra—the Grevy's zebra and the mountain zebra—are endangered. Fortunately, zebras are now protected by law from hunters. And some lands have been set aside as preserves for zebras and other animals.

But big cattle herds still compete with zebras for food and water. Farmers also drain water from rivers for crops.

Scientists and other people are working with Africa's farmers and herders to help protect zebras and their habitat. That way, the "tiger-horses" will always have a home to roam.

Fast Facts About Plains Zebras

Scientific name	*Equus burchelli*
Class	Mammals
Order	Perissodactyla
Size	4 to 5 feet tall at shoulders
Weight	Males to 900 pounds; Females to 500 pounds
Life span	About 18 years in the wild About 30 years in captivity
Habitat	Grasslands and savannas
Top speed	About 40 miles per hour

The Horse Family

Zebras are part of a scientific family called *Equidae*. This family includes domestic horses, wild horses called tarpans and Przewalski's horses, as well as donkeys and their wild cousins.

Glossary of Wild Words

bray   to make loud sounds like those of a donkey

colt   a young male zebra

filly   a young female zebra

foal   a baby zebra

genus   a large category of related plants or animals consisting of smaller groups (**species**) of closely related plants or animals

graze   to eat grass

grooming   cleaning of fur, skin, or feathers by an animal

habitat   the natural environment where an animal or plant lives

mane   hair growing along the back of an animal's neck

mare   an adult female zebra

nurse	to feed a baby animal with milk from the mother's breast	**savanna**	a flat grassland with trees in a warm area of the world
plain	a large, flat area of dry land; a grassland	**species**	a group of plants or animals that are the same in many ways
predator	an animal that hunts and eats other animals to survive	**stallion**	an adult male zebra
preserves	areas of land or water where wildlife and plants are protected	**wildebeest**	another word for a gnu, an antelope that looks a bit like an ox with big, curved horns

Index